© 2022. Mia Burley. All rights reserved.
No part of this book may be reproduced, or stored in a retrieval system, or transmitted in any form or by any means, electronic, mechanical, photocopying, recording, or otherwise, without express written permission of the publisher.

ISBN: 978-1-3999-3847-1

Cover design by: Chloe Darnill
Internal design by: Mia Burley
Printed in the United Kingdom

The characters and events portrayed in this book are fictitious. Any similarity to real persons, living or dead, is coincidental and not intended by the author.

The Wisdom Life Gave You

Mia Burley

To all who need to be seen.

Quiet Awakening

There is a luxury in silence that can't quite truly be defined.
A moment of stillness that reaches even the most overactive mind.
And yet;
The absence of noise it is not.
Instead,
A sacred opportunity to hear for the very first time.

The Temple Gates

There is a cavern inside of me,
A depth even I haven't yet reached.
It holds more than I could excavate in a lifetime,
More than anyone could possibly comprehend.

There is a darkness inside of me,
A night that lasts for eternity.
A nothingness from which both creation and destruction wield their miracles.

There is a power inside of me,
A force of 1000 archetypes.
Maiden, Mother, Wild Woman, Crone.
Their wisdom, their stories, their perspectives,
All woven together in my internal throne.

There is a Priestess inside of me,
A presence that is felt but often unheard.
Who's work and service requires no words.
Who's touch can leave you empowered and undone.

There is a Witch inside of me,
A magick as old as time.
A resilience that's only ever fueled by fire,
Who gathers her sisters, her herbs and her tinctures,
And marches to the beat of her own homemade drum.

There is a whole Universe inside of me,
Planets that collide and constellations that guide.
The fabric of my innocence, initiations, pleasure and pain.
The tapestry of lifetimes in the tiniest of rooms.

My teacher.
My alchemist.
My womb.

When Did You Forget To Dream?

That dream you had, when you were a child,
The one you left behind, casting it aside as far too wild,
It still calls to you, doesn't it? From deep within.
Well let me tell you something,
It's time to begin..

To reconnect with that effortless joy,
To remember life through the lens of innocence and coy,
To let that young one lead you to a time more free,
To let your past guide your present,
If you get quiet, you'll hear her plea..

"When did you forget to dream?" She'll say;
"You know magic is real when you let yourself play.
There's no such thing as pipe dreams, or make believe to avoid the real world.
Don't you remember it's make believe that creates and designs YOUR world?

When did you get caught up in the lie?
And only ever think of me with a despondent sigh?
We used to have it all, you and me, even at the tender age of 3.
Before they told you that you can't,
Before tests and grades began dictating your path,
Before false responsibility fell upon your shoulder,
There was a time when you were so much bolder.

Bold enough to dream fantasy into reality,
Young enough to see it all with total clarity,
There was a time when you had the audacity to believe it was possible,
I'm telling you now, it's actually probable.

*When you let yourself dream in the way that we used to,
Let your imagination take over, create and leave clues; for the next generation, so they never get swept up,
In this culture of defiance of their own inner pup.
Let the children lead, they really do know,
How to bring the world back to sparkle and glow."*

The Whole In Your Heart

How's your heart today?
Have you asked yourself yet?
Do you take the time to reflect,
Or do you mostly forget?

How do you actually feel today?
In this chaotic world of contradiction,
Do you know?
Or are you painting on a smile again to avoid unnecessary friction?

How would you like to be seen today?
If there was someone who would witness you, wholly and fully.
If you could lay yourself bare and trust you wouldn't have to run from the bully that is this warped reality of decorum and keeping up appearances.

How would you like to be valued today?
If vulnerability was currency and unconditional acceptance this season's hottest product?
Would you cash in those chips stored up in your heart, unlocking all emotions and embracing the part,

that each of them play in making you, you.

Like lost jigsaw pieces finally completing the picture,
Of not just your 'good side',

but the
    whole,
        messy,
            mixture.

Full. Empty. Alive

'What do you want, dear Soul?' She whispered,

I want to love endlessly, yet break my heart just to know how it feels.
I want euphoria at every turn, but not without desperate depression, just to recognise the difference.

I want to be scared this belly of ours may burst if I laugh any harder,
And I want to worry these eyes may dissolve if I cry any longer.
This body I'm in, it's capable of so much.
The most decadent sensations at the slightest touch.
I want to know its farthest limits and I want to know it's delectable comfort.

My only wish is that you allow it all,
Please try not to run from, or avoid.
I want to go to extremes, and I want to dwell for a while in the void.

The richness of contrast is so understated,
The wealth in duality so very underrated.
I want you to see the value in every feeling,
To witness the sheer depth of the human condition,
To know the shift from doubt to believing,
From terror to faith,
From emptiness to empathy,
From envy to self recognition,
From nervous to radiant.
And back again.
I want it all.

Do not be afraid of the full spectrum of emotion.
This is all my way of saying;
I just want to be human.

Choose

Choose to see, see it all.
See into different worlds, different timelines, alternative realities.
Choose to see behind, in front, all around.
You can.
So easily in fact, that you miss it when you try.
You don't need to try.
You just, see.

A Happy Middle

Wake me up
Shake me up
Show me what it takes to walk through my
days with the type of awareness that moves
mountains and initiates earthquakes.

Hand me the mirror so that I may catch a
glimmer
      of the truth inside me that can shatter
illusions…
            and replenish the Earth's lakes…
with water clean enough to wash away
the willful ignorance of a species dependent on
governing insolence.

Bathe us in cognitive dissonance and rinse off
the ease of blissful innocence.

Let us all smell the coffee that has long been
stale
And find it within ourselves to post our own bail
      from this prison of safety and
outsourced responsibility.

Let us find our way home, look hard, our ancestors left a trail.
And once we're there, let us find a balance.
A cradle of oneness that creates harmony at last.

Let the pendulum settle once and for all,

In a happy middle.

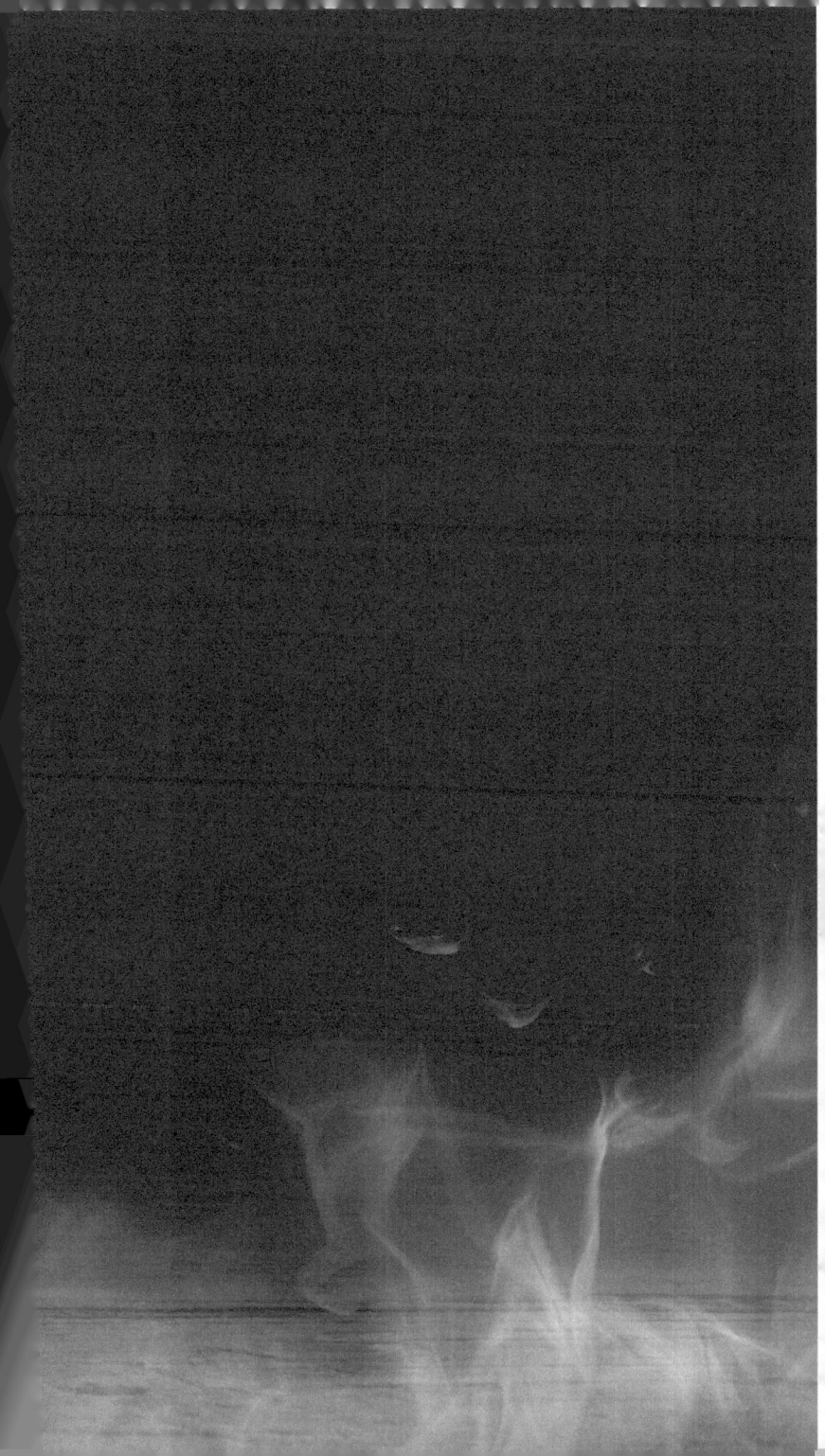

Vanishing Act

And then she disappeared.
As quickly as she was there, she no longer was.
The easiest type of exit.
The type no-one notices,
or at least can tell themselves they didn't.
Life returns to normal, as though the upset never occurred.
As though routines were never interrupted, the status quo never disrupted.
And all is as it was.
Quiet.
Unchallenged.
Safe.
Safe in the knowledge that the toxicity can once again be covered.
Hidden beneath the lies we tell ourselves in the shower misted mirror every morning.
Because the real mirror was too harsh for prolonged eye contact.
So you look away.
And she disappears.

You Are Enough

You are allowed to flow, so flow.
You are enough

You don't need to force the outcome, so relax.
You are enough

Your words have impact, your presence is felt, your gift is always working, even when you are not.
You are enough

You are allowed to take up space, how do you expect to expand if you don't create the room to grow into?
You are enough

You arrived here with built in phases for action and for rest.
You are enough. In every phase.

You are allowed to let miracles in, in fact it's imperative that you do.
You are enough

You are allowed to let others take the lead, you don't have to be in control all the time, let trust in.
You are enough

You are magnificence, beauty, power and grace, even when you are simply being.
You are enough

You are limitless when you rest and unstoppable when you move.
You are enough

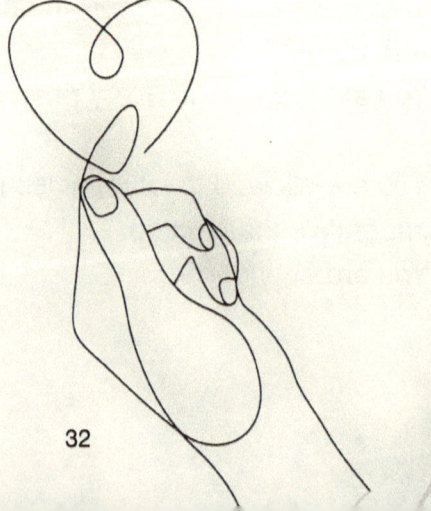

Witness Yourself

Don't forget to win sometimes,
In this game you play against yourself.
Don't forget to pepper in some ladders
amongst those snakes,
And take that self esteem down off the shelf.
It deserves pride of place, as do you.
And recognition for all that you do.
Witness yourself first for all that you are,
And know you don't have to constantly keep
raising the bar.
Sometimes it's ok to just truly see,
The wholeness of you today, and let yourself
be.

Fall For Yourself

I love you so damn much, more than you'll ever know.
And my love for you is only ever going to grow.
Through fields and trees and across the ocean blue,
I can't believe for all this time, you never had a clue.

I'm so damn proud of you, sometimes I think I may burst,
That after all these years, you're finally putting yourself first.
I'm so happy for you, and happy for me,
Happy for US, thank you for setting us both free..
From friends who were false and from opinions that don't matter,
From self critiques and the internal batter,
From doubting your worth, your talent and your gifts,
This next chapter, my love, you will not want to miss.
The floor is now yours and the stage is now set,

These mid years of the adventure will be your best yet.
And I'll be right with you, every step of the way,
Guiding you, loving you, applauding you as I pray;
That now we're in this together, you'll never look back,
That we co-steer this ship to eternity, and you keep hearing me say;

I love you, my human, thank you for letting me lead,
This old Soul will never get tired, but I'm glad I no longer have to plead.
So let's go forth together and conquer our destiny,
With confidence, with finesse, never forgetting humility.
Let's show them how it's done, and maybe one day, they too,
Will feel that deep love, that crossed the ocean blue.

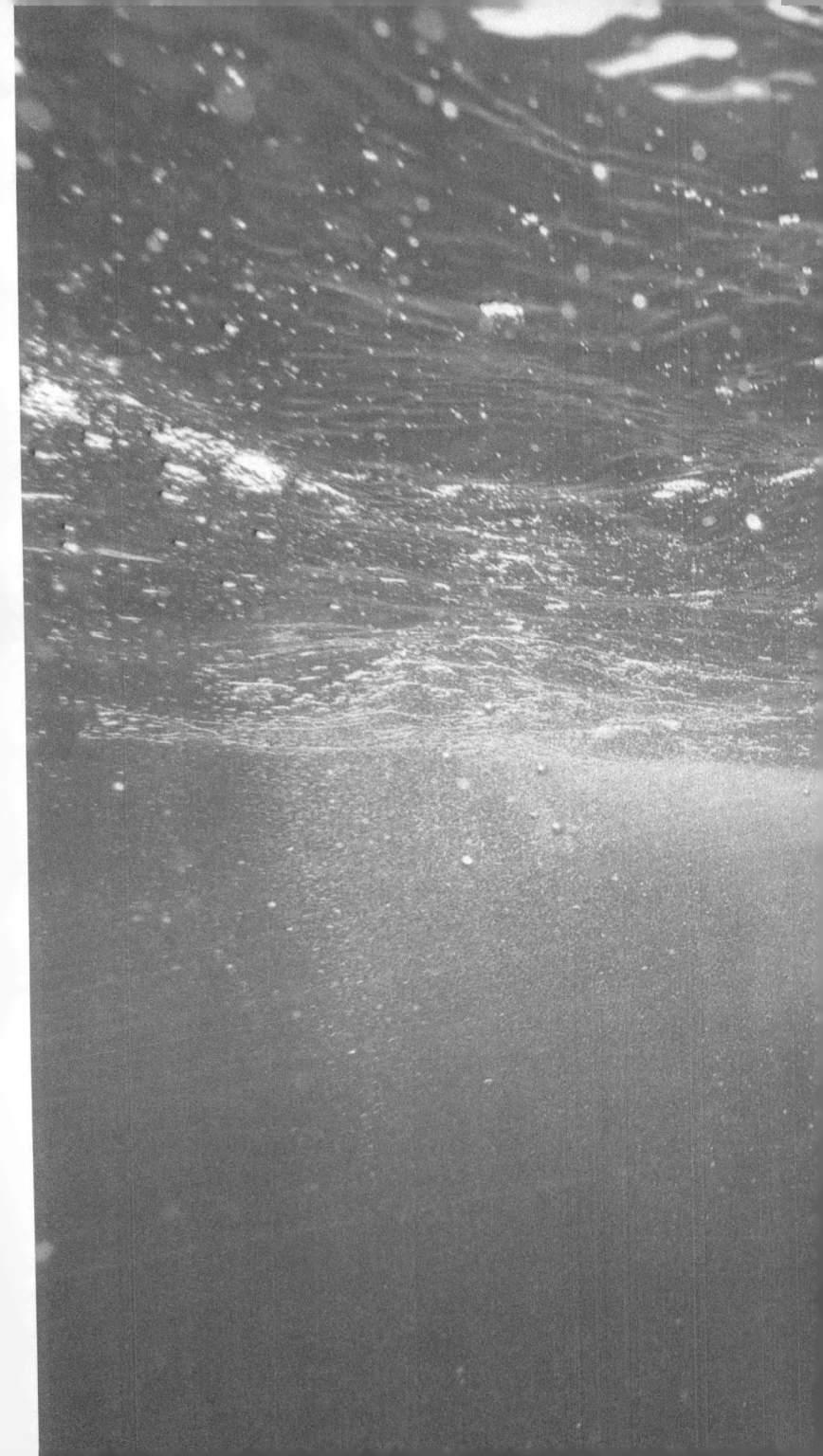

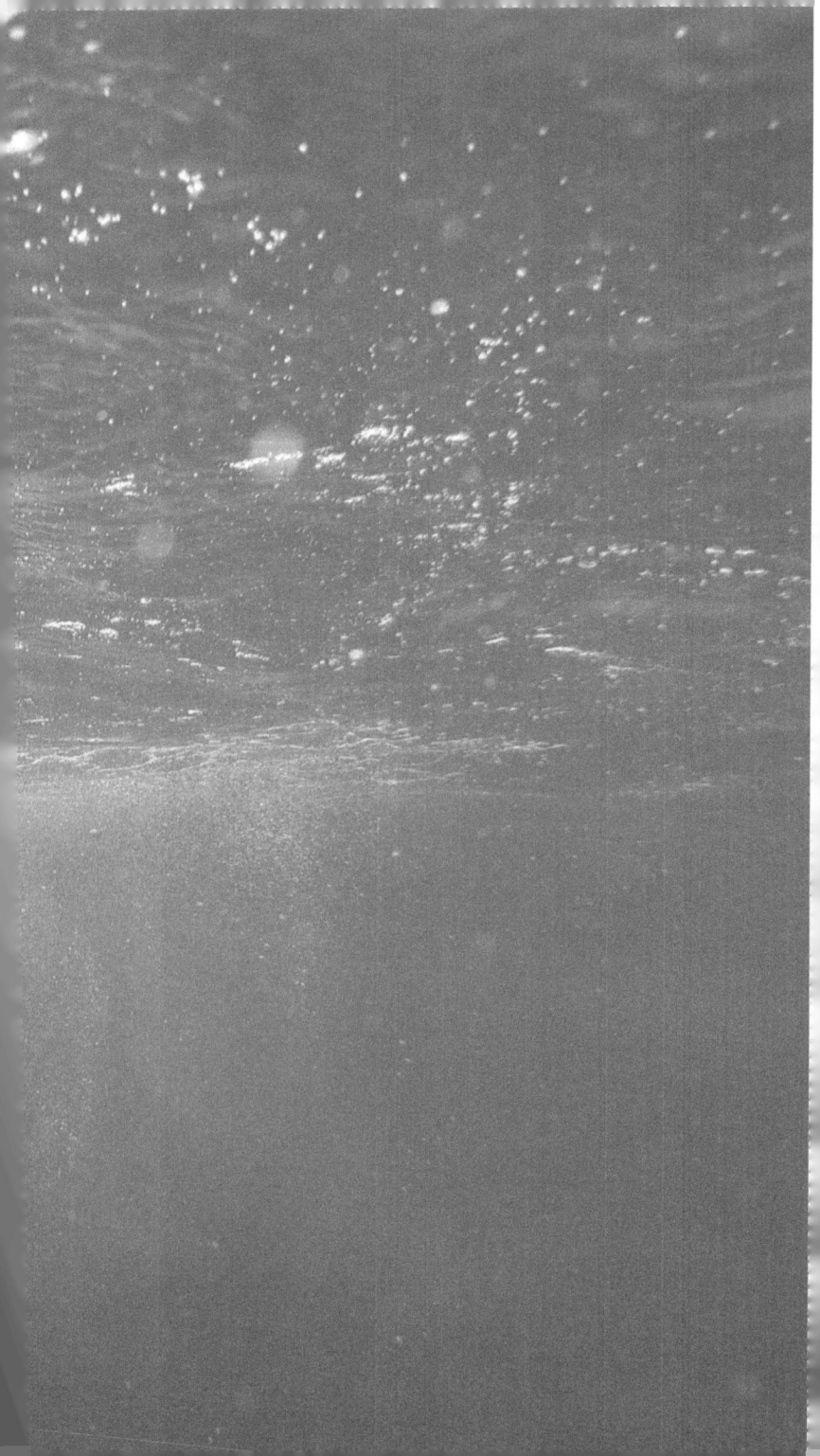

Second Guessing

Did I make it real too soon?
Is there now too much pressure for it all to bloom?
Why does it suddenly feel like there's an expectation,
To meet deadlines and quotas and rush to completion?
There was once an ease and a joy that now feels stunted.
Replaced with stories that don't need to be told.
Determination disgruntled.

Having It All

It's in the simplest moments that you realise;
happiness found you.
It's in the miraculous mundane that you
realise; there's no chase required.
That happiness is fleeting
And yet all consuming
All of the time and none of the time.

It's in the acoustic guitar that plays whilst your
love completes a chore and you sip coffee.
It's in the breeze through the window that
ushers in the winter sun.
It's in the smile that comes from within when
you find yourself in a moment of "this is
enough".

And you pause;
suspended in time,
experiencing it all,
this moment of being alive

These are the moments you remember forever.
These are the times that make you realise how lucky you are.
These are the moments that humble you to the ecstasy of simplicity.

Blind Self Love

Love is gentle, and love is kind,
But love, so often, can leave you blind.
Those blinkers you've worn to forgive all manner of sins,
May you apply them to yourself and unleash your own wins.

Keep your wits about you when you look for a partner,
But rose tinted glasses are the key to happily ever after;
When you look in the mirror.

If you can look past their red flags, you can look beyond your insecurities,
If you can ignore their warning signs, you can move forward in spite of your own perceived inferiorities.
That love you give to those who don't receive it with grace,
Turn it back on yourself, and in that space;
Receive the magic of seeing yourself through the eyes of another,
The one who's blinded by your beauty and your talent, all aflutter,

Be so intoxicated on the fumes of your own worth,
Your inner critic lays to rest as ashes on your internal hearth,
And in the fire that alchemised society's harsh gaze,
A power rises, ushering in a new phase;

Of blind acceptance, but not at the compromise of your value,
Of unquestioning forgiveness,
but this time it's you who atones,
For all manner of sins committed in the desire for validation,
Repented
on the altar
of YOU.

Love is gentle, and love is unconditional.
May you receive with grace from the warm embrace,
Of your own, rose tinted glasses wearing, heart.

Your Words Matter

Let it all out.

Let it all fall
      and tumble
           and express
                and SCREAM

                    and FINALLY

                    be

                        heard.

Let the voice that was silenced,
made fun of,
disregarded,
put down
and made to feel irrelevant finally have her say.

Let

her

fucking

roar.

Let her anger be known.
Let her hurt and disappointment be felt.
She can *not* be contained any longer.

Can you do that?

Can you say it's all ok?

Or do you ache for another chance to have those precious, sacred years again, with the wisdom, courage and support you have now?

Your words matter.

Your voice matters.

Your perspective matters.

Do not be spoken over anymore.
Do not be reduced to the silent, willing, good girl.
Do not sacrifice your spirit for 10 seconds of absent approval.

Growing Pains

Fear comes up when you're on the right path,
My darling, look it straight in the face and laugh.
Do not mistake it as a warning sign for danger,
This is so different to footsteps too close from a stranger.

This is the feeling that tells of growth,
Of stepping out of comfort,
And claiming more courage than most;
To do what's really on your heart and follow the nudges of your Soul,
Saying 'yes' to this voice is your one and only goal.

The fear is real, but welcome it and lean in,
You'll soon meet another feeling, it's next of kin,
Those butterflies of nerves begin to transform,
And suddenly FAITH courses through you, delicate and warm.

The two together are the ultimate weapon,
Defending your dreams as you work to make them happen,
Run towards your fears and your faith will have your back,
As you prove to yourself there is nothing you lack.

What you're meant to fulfill through pure Divine Will starts to materialise from the moment you say;
YES, I'm ready now. I may not know how and I may not know the way,
But I know what I'm supposed to be, so I'll be it, and I'll pray.

When You Fall

Falling on rocky times,
Falling further still, to rock bottom,
And then falling once more.
The times when all you could do was sit and stare,
The pain of existing too much to bear.
They happened more often than you expected or thought possible,
14 years of bungee jumping between hope and desperate sorrow.
Diagnoses, pills, wards and police stations,
Where the Soul goes to die, and the human really tries.
It would have been so easy to let go.
But something inexplicable,
Unidentifiable,
Said no.
And now here we are, awake and alive.
With a resilience unbreakable, ready for whatever 'aliveness' throws.
Reincarnated within the same lifespan.
Able to hold it all.
And catch you.
When you fall.

The Manifesto of Me

More joy, more rest, more putting myself first,
No longer will I uphold this curse.

I will challenge myself daily to be the least impressive version of myself,
and marvel at the genius that arises from the captives of my own impossible standard.

Create without expectation and know that when a masterpiece is not required, it is miraculously delivered.

No longer will meaningless tasks be completed at the expense of myself in an attempt to demonstrate worth already proven by the fact I have air in my lungs and blood in my veins.

I will be so unwavering in my own power and my own values that nothing and no-one can compromise them.

I will be so grounded in my own energy that anything and anyone who doesn't match ricochets off me into memory and eventually irrelevance.

Life's resilience training finally rising through me as I become unapologetic in my loyalty to myself.

Call me selfish if you must.
Call me entitled if it allows you to feel more comfortable with my presence.
But no longer will the opinions of others create a space where my very essence is up for negotiation.

You're A Bit Sensitive

Change your environment, change your life.
It's either feeding you or sucking you dry.
There's no in between, not for someone as sensitive as you.
That sensitivity is a super power by the way.
I can't wait for you to realise this.

The Radiance of The Everyday Queen

To the Queen who feels like anything but; you are radiant.

To the Queen who questions herself more often than she'd care to admit; you are more sovereign than you realise.

To the Queen who can feel as though she has nothing to offer and is on her last legs; let those legs buckle, I promise your power will catch you.

To the Queen who has everything and nothing figured out; you are so seen, and so recognised, and so loved.

To the Queen who's humility can sometimes morph into harsh self critique; know that you don't need to have all the answers, for this is a Queendom, and you're surrounded by crowns.

Let ALL the Queens come together. Not to sit at the feet of an oracle but to collectively become the oracle.
To remember a time when we were in this together; supporting, celebrating, crying, laughing and loving.

Let the leaders come together. Not to hear the latest tricks of the trade to pass down to your followers, but to relinquish all connection to hierarchy and remember how to lead by living.

Let the women come together. Not in faux feminism or secret competition, but as independent power houses of soft and gentle wisdom, ready and willing to come undone.
To pick apart the last stitches of the moth eaten fabric of the patriarchy and join together in true collaboration, so that everybody wins.

The Tired Muse

I'm content today, but I love that you still want to play.
Your commitment to the page that releases me from my cage is noble and humble and for that I say 'hooray'.
But today I slumber in a grateful rest,
So take a break, my love, do not put me to the test.
You can rely on me as I know I can rely on you,
To show up with the pen and receive the words that flow through.
It's ok to wait, it's ok to take your time.
We're a good team, you and me.
Some may say we're in our prime.
So don't stress for today,
Put down the tools and find another way to play,
I'll be back before you know it.

Ghosts

The days drag on,
My heart desperate to hear a
different song.
But this limbo continues,
for months so long.
All I want is to finally be gone.

Gone from the place that I hold in
disgrace,
Full of stale old memories and the
worn out face,
Of the corpse of a version of me that
no longer breathes, but has not yet been laid
to rest, and so she seethes.

As the newer me is dying to be born,
Caught in the middle, between two worlds torn.
A new beginning, dependent on an ending that just won't quit.

Held captive in this game of waiting.
The future imagination, the past a shadow.
The present a ghost, at an all time low.

Are you ready?

If there was ever a question with a more impossible answer.

Readiness is an illusionary concept used to create a sense of safety in the unknown.
The truth is we can never be ready for an experience we've never had before because the experience will always be different to how the limited human mind can anticipate it.
Readiness traps you in over thinking.
Start asking if you're willing.

Willing to try.

Willing to fail.

Willing to keep going.

Willing to move forward.

Willing to grow.

Willing to expand.

Willing to invite in the experience that's necessary for you right now.

You miss so much of life when you wait to be ready.

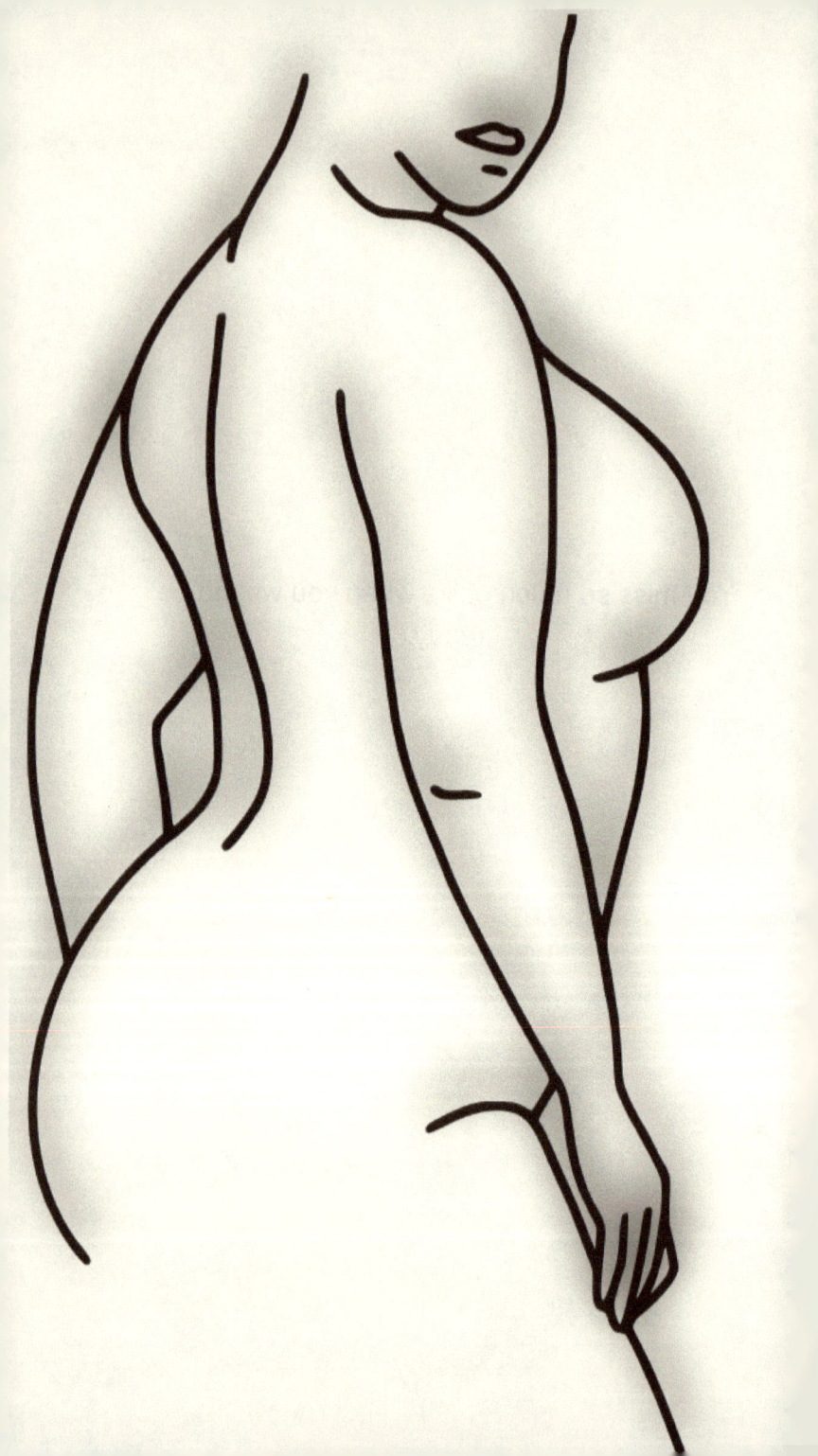

There Are Worse Things You Can Be Than Fat

Question:

Why is "fat" the worst thing you can be?

Why are we all so damn scared of putting on weight?

Answer:

Because we're terrified society will treat us differently if we do.

THAT is the crisis that needs addressing.

There are worse things you can be than fat.

Death of The Martyr

Not giving to yourself first is a pain you will no longer tolerate.
You are a pioneer, not a martyr.
The work looks different when you forge your own path.
There are no rules, because no-one has walked these steps before in order to create them.
You can not get it wrong, because no-one has gone before you to get it right.
It is you,
with you,
figuring it out as you go along,
FOR you.

How beautiful a world where we all do this without questioning.
There is so much that we do not question;
yet our own wisdom, desires, ideas, choices, self expression are pulled apart by the internal jury of doubt.

When did you decide the truth of another was more valid and real than the truth of you?
When did you decide that what you know had to be validated by people with more perceived power than you?
What's inside you is more than valid,
It's necessary.
It's the whole reason you have a heart that beats and a voice that speaks.

Your Soul deemed it valid enough to jump into a body and spend all these Earth years sharing it.

And yet you question yourself?

Mary's Advice

"Everything's alright, yes, everything's fine"
You do know this don't you?
You do know that this is an immortal truth, no matter what's going on?

Tell me ONE time it has ever not been alright?

So how about you give yourself a break?
How about you just be present today?
Don't look for advice, don't look for things to change, don't look to understand and analyse everything so you can have an explanation for your feelings.

How about you just feel them?

Allow them to take you on this rollercoaster of a human experience and know that everything is STILL alright.
You can still have joy, gratitude, fulfillment, overflow even when it feels like your tear ducts are running dry and your heart can be pinched no tighter.

It is never either or.
It is both.
It is them all.
It is life.

"Everything's alright yes, everything's fine".
Just for today, don't try to change anything.

Just live.

Let The Darkness Come

Let Divinity pour through me.
Let wisdom wash over me,
cascading through my consciousness like a
Lumerian waterfall.

Let me fall apart.
Let the paradigms of the past,
the worn out ways,
the stale status quo,
be gently but rapidly flushed from my being.

Let me step into the new, fully initiated by the collapse of society.
The embodiment of the teachings of grief.
Let my mourning for everything I once knew be the platform from which evolution is born.

A woman undone, a woman with nothing to lose, a woman who does not fear the depths of her own despair,
Who confronts the darkest parts of her psyche and sees them reflected in the darkness of the world.

This is woman rising.
This is the woman who knows broken doesn't mean to be without use or purpose.
On the contrary, this woman knows it is only when we break that we see a better way to build.

Let the darkness close around me, for it is here that I see most clearly.
Here that I hear most profoundly.
Here that I am safe to let the broken parts of me fall away.
Where I am held and supported whilst I receive their wisdom.

Let the darkness engulf me, for it is here that I find acceptance.
It is here that I stop resisting.
Here that I allow all that will be to be and remember it has no bearing on the life I decide to live.

In the darkness, choices appear.
Choices bigger and more varied than you ever imagined.
But you are required to make them blindly.
You are required to make them with your heart and your Soul and you allow your faith to guide you.
To allow your faith to lead you back to the light, knowing the darkness will come again, fearing it less each time.

Until the day you look forward to it,
Until the day when you welcome the descent.
And you realise the darkness reveals to you what you are made of.
A sacred initiation that proves you can hold it all.

That uncovers strength in vulnerability.
Connection in solitude.
Clarity in chaos.

In the darkness, you remember your magic.
You perform alchemy with your words.
Artistry with your pain.
Power with your presence.

Stormy Weather

The storms rage outside like they rage inside my mind,
You'll never know the damage you caused by being so unkind.

Sometimes I wonder if you came out unscathed,
Or if the reality of your actions eventually brought your own psyche to cave.

They say those who perpetrate hurt are the ones who hurt most themselves,
As though we are expected to excuse all lethal behaviour and instead simply show compassion for our neighbour.

But once hurt, you now have a choice;
To pass on those wounds with your fists and your voice,
Or to spend the rest of your life with one endeavour,
To ensure YOU are never the cause of someone's inner extreme weather.

Joy

Joy is the one thing they can never take.
As long as you realise you hold the power to create it.
As long as you know it's available in every breath, every heartbeat, every smile.
As your Dad used to say; "The best revenge is your happiness. Show them they had no effect on you whatsoever".
Joy is a necessary skill in a world that thrives off of misery.

Dead Soul Walking

Blood rushing through my ears to the tune of my heart.
Begging me to pay attention, to listen, to actually make a start.
On all the things I long for but never dared to acknowledge,
Too scared to fail, to make a scene, or to deal with regret under the heat of the spotlight.

But the regret of not trying at all begins to pinch tight,
The roaring of my heart louder with every missed flight,
        of opportunity to overcome the mediocrity of an accepted norm,
To show humanity a way out of the storm,
        of depressing routine and Soul crushing 9-5's,

We're living, but my God, we're not alive.

That heart that beats in your chest wants so much more,
There's a whole world to witness, to experience and explore,
And time for it all, if we drop the 40 hours of prison,
Instead opting for community service of connecting and sharing our wisdom,

Imagine what we could build together if we'd only make a start.
So pay attention,
And listen to that heart.

Raw Power

When you sit with your womb, you sit with God.
You sit with the true essence of power as it is supposed to be experienced,
Sans the corruption.

When you listen to your womb, you finally hear silence,
Filled with deep wisdom and knowing.

She has so much to say, and she WILL be heard.
Though rarely will she say it with words.

She can not be ignored with pills full of fake hormones and she can not be plugged up and pushed through, oh my, will you feel her groans.

She will love you even though you've been taught to hate her,
But she will get increasingly mad at the patriarchy as it continues to berate her.
And you will feel this madness, between your thighs.
Every twist and cramp and bitter deep sigh.
And you'll wonder what you did to deserve this curse.
Until finally you sit with her, and SHE reveals your purpose.

And suddenly you realise why they're so scared,
Why for such brutal suppression of this power they are prepared.
Why they won't allow her to be fairly studied,
Why ripping her out is the one and only solution they arrive at in a flurry.
Why the owners of wombs are the subject of such duress,
Left misrepresented yet expected to clear up this mess.

Once returned to your knowing,
you throw your head back
and laugh,
Throw the pills in the bin
and return to your path,
Of raw power,
in its truest essence,
Of witch's wisdom
in your fertile possession.

When you sit with your womb, you sit with God.

God is a woman, with a devoted Jesus between her legs.

THAT'S why they're scared.

Fre(M)Edom

Screw 'I am enough'. I am ME.
Take all your affirmations back, I am ME.
Take all your projections back, I am ME.

I do not explain my wild and free emotions away with 'childhood trauma';
Condemning them to over analysis and long, drawn out 'healing' so I can appear on the world's stage the perfect performer.
Why do I need to be anything other than ME?
Oh the irony of affirming 'I am enough' in the hope that I become something different to the beautiful, sacred mess of inconsistency I am and always will be.

Take back your 'tapping', your commodified spirituality I do flee,
I am a miracle in a body. I am ME.
I do not want your psycho analysis, leave my experiences alone.
The joyous,
The crazy,
The heartbreaking,
The hilarious,

The loving,
The terrifying,
The life changing.
They are mine. And I am ME.

I will not be industrialised with a 6 step system and a hefty fee,
Offering my heart on a plate and my trust on a tray because you told me you'd take my fear and scarcity away.
You may keep your secrets to success and your filtered 'life goals'.
I am too busy living;
Unfiltered,
Unapologetic,
Unashamed.

I am too busy being ME, without explanation.
I am too busy being ME, loving and hating my creations.
I am too busy being ME, full of duality and contradiction.
I am too busy being ME, shedding comparison and competition.

I am too busy being ME, embracing all experiences and emotions.
I am too busy being ME, kicking up a huge commotion.

So take it all back, I don't need it anymore.
I borrowed it for a while, but my authenticity got sore.
So you do you, and I'll be me.
Because I realise now, that's all I need to be free.

Uncomfortably One

To L-I-V-E is to witness E-V-I-L.
In yourself.
In those you know.
In those who are far away but who's actions affect the whole world.

We love to think it's separate from us, but it isn't.
It's right there, encapsulated in our human experience, waiting to see if the switch will be flicked in this lifetime.

You may catch glimpses of it in the otherwise well intentioned from time to time,
A harsh word, an unjust behaviour, an apology that took too long or lacked integrity.
You may observe it posing as the friendly neighbourhood watch guru, condemning without context under the guise of social justice.

And you certainly see it in our leaders, who aren't really leaders at all.

You can not deny its existence in the world,
So you can not deny its existence in you.

Witness yourself as much as you witness your surroundings.
Be willing to accept the reflections from the global hall of mirrors.

Allow it to guide you to compassion, empathy and understanding.
There is no antidote to E-V-I-L, because there is no antidote to your responsibility to L-I-V-E.
But perhaps with the acceptance of it, we might be half way there.
The more you see the atrocities "out there".
The more you're invited to love the atrocities "in here".

Home

Home really was here all along,
In these bones, in this body.
I searched relentlessly in others,
Hoping to find familiarity under the covers,
But the separation and isolation would always reappear with the morning gong.

Comfort was really right here all the time,
In these soft curves, in this work of art.
I looked high and low, across filters and procedures,
But in the end, nothing quite hit the spot like loving this temple of mine.

Acceptance was really right here in front of me,
In the eyes that stare back from the mirror,
The look of loving appreciation, breaking away from societal gaze.
I chased it with shakes, with meetings and starvation,
With enough physical activity to injure a whole nation,
But the 'points' I scored were never enough,
The goal posts moved with every new craze.

The answer was simple, in the end.
When you stop trying to change, to mold and to bend.
When you feed yourself to nourish,
When you fill yourself up with courage,
And finally say 'No' to the norm of self rejection.

It was all in you, right from the start,
In these legs, in these arms, in this big beautiful heart.
Home, comfort, acceptance and love.
No more searching now, of that, you are above.

The Gift of Silence

In a world where everyone shouts and tells
you what you "should" be doing, get silent.

Do not project your trauma, guilt or misplaced
responsibility outwards through unintentional
and ungrounded noise.

Get quiet.

Dare to meet yourself.
Dare to sit in the way the air feels,
the way your breath feels,
the way your body feels.
Let the only noise you hear be the beat of your
own heart,
and listen to it until it forms words, poems,
songs, truth.

Your response is not out there,
your contribution not a thoughtless share.
When you feel the exasperation reside,
turn around and take an intentional stride,
Away from the noise,
into your own chamber,
Where nothing awaits, but everything lays
bare.

Where you remember your own wisdom, from the past, present and future,
Where true healing lies, and you finally stop tearing out the suture.

There is such powerful action in raw, honest inaction.
The pause you take, whilst the rest of the world quakes,
That's the moment you do more,
contribute more,
participate more than you ever could imagine.

My darling, let the buzzwords go,
Let them fall away and allow silence to grow.
The answer sounds different upon each ear,
and continues to transmute year after year.

So let it unfold as a story untold and allow the stillness to dissipate the fear.
Do not make noise for the simple sake of noise.
What needs to be said will, at the right moment, become clear.

The Heartbreak That Saved Me

Empty and alone, but craving your touch,
Not understanding why I want you so much.
So clever you are, to entwine my heart with yours,
To have softened my defenses each time I took pause.

Knowing deep down this could only ever end in tears,
Yet, if it wasn't for you, I may not even be here.
Such a twisted angel you are to have been my saviour who couldn't stay.
To have given me so much, only to take it all away.
To let me one day discover that it was never yours to give.

So talented you are to have trapped me this way,
To have silenced my alarm bells with such expert grace.
To save my life, but break my heart,
With the combined force of all those who did depart.

Your shadow will forever remain imprinted on my aura,
In equal parts gratitude and disgust.
The Dark Knight who rode into The Dark Night of my Soul,

Who fixed me, and then broke me so hard I had no choice but to learn how to make myself whole.

Thank you.
And fuck you.

Slow Down

Stop rushing my love, this isn't a race.
Give yourself the gift of your own authentic pace.
Do you even know what it is you're trying to complete?
Or are you simply caught up in pressure to compete?

We are not cars on a race track attempting the fastest time,
We are people with an opportunity to make life sublime.
You can do that when you slow down and appreciate each day,
For exactly what it is, even the ones that make you look around in dismay.

What are you trying to get finished so fast?
It's all life.
There's always more to come.
There's no deadline.
Only a dead line.
And I'm pretty sure you're not ready to pass.

Starting Over

Strip yourself back, undo it all.
Become naked in front of a world cloaked in not self.
Forget so that you might once more remember,
Blank it all out,
Make everything irrelevant.
Start again, from day one.
And this time, own it.

#BeKind

Right now I have nothing enlightened to share,
Only the pain on my heart to bear.
I have no big epiphanies that fly out of difficulties,
Only grief, and the burden of care.

Trying to find balance between too much and not enough,
There comes a time when it's too exhausting to stay tough.
The days when you question if it's even worth it,
Or if it would be better to just sleep in, and let them win.

The era of #BeKind but always too late,
Where traits become trends, get lost and seal our fate.
Wandering No Man's Land, an open target,
So easily seen, but just as easy to forget.

Once the shot has been fired and hit where it hurts,
Only the recoil is tended to, prepping to assert.
Everywhere you turn, the swords are drawn,
And what was once so open and loving is now forlorn.

What to show, and what to keep hidden?
The endless plight to try and stay driven.
So right now, I have no clear message to share.
But please #BeKind, I know deep down you all still care.

Did You Know?

You can make light of it, you know, this thing
called life.

You ARE light you know, capable of shining
through all kinds of strife.

You can be fun and silly, you know,
Turns out there's lots more guarantees than
just death and taxes.

So promise me something please,
ENJOY yourself as the patriarchy collapses.

The Illusionist

Nothing comes from everything, and everything comes from nothing.
You are the sum of all your parts and a fresh slate all at the same time.
You are paradoxical by nature and that's what makes this Earth mission so exciting.

As you move forward each day, shedding distractions,
leaving behind the parts of you that were asleep, and the physical mirrors of the versions of you that no longer exist,
you become nothing and everything all at the same time.

Death happens everyday. Rebirth happens everyday.

These are very indifferent things that humanity has attached meaning to so that the beauty of them goes unnoticed.
Attaching meaning to things denies them of their own truth.

Attaching meaning to things coats them in a filter of narratives that become lost in translation,
the very reason they were gifted in the first place vanishes.

But that's ok, because nothing is everything and everything is nothing.

You have the power to reset,
alchemise,
re-write,
change direction,

at any moment.

You get to play with the illusions in front of you,
make the fragmented light hit a different angle
and watch it become something else entirely.

Nothing and everything.
Doesn't that set you free?

Context Cancelled

Is anyone saying anything authentic?
This cancel culture is so pathetic.
Stifling creatives and threatening the word.
I've never witnessed anything so bloody absurd.

Has humanity forgotten all nuance and context?
That the experience behind the expression is so much more complex?
That a person's full spectrum of beliefs and perspective span so much further than this tiny collective,
Of phrases that are pulled apart and assassinated with unintended meaning.

You are missing the point of being alive,
And robbing yourself of depth in an empty effort to contrive,
A world where feelings never get hurt,
Oh, I just found something even more absurd.

Words

The greatest gift is the gift of our sound,
Our very own c(h)ords where vocal melodies are found.
Do we truly understand the power in our voice?
The instrument that casts spells every time we open our mouths,
and declare our choice,
       of words to flow from thought to reality?

If we did, perhaps we'd pick them more carefully.

Looks may kill, but words will start wars.
They'll lead nations into battle and bring destruction to the Earth's core.
Words can break hearts and shatter dreams,
And change the course of one's life with one damning scene.

They break far more than bones,
move over sticks and stones,
the right words will tear apart the Spirit,
building walls of perceived protection that leave you cold and alone.

Those cords in our throat will end friendships in an instant,
Revealing the truth of manipulation behind an illusion of meaningful connection.

They can even cause illness, poverty and depression.
Yes, if we really knew the power of them, we'd make things look very different.

But words can also heal like nothing else,
And open that heart back up to love,
Cracking you wide open and spilling over,
tipping the scales in fortuitous favour.

The right words, printed and bound, can reach straight into your Soul and see you in ways you've always wanted to be seen,
They can spark tears of joy all the way from stage to screen.

They can find new friendships, with people in the know, of the power of words, who use them only to help you glow.
They create connections far deeper than before,
When they give a voice to a shared experience.

The greatest gift is the gift of our word, let's use it to bring healing to the Earth at its core.

Parting Wisdom

Other people will rarely understand your happiness.
That's fine.

Be happy anyway.

Go where you need to go.
Do what you need to do.
Never compromise your happiness to keep people in the room with you.

Never dampen your joy so they can make you make sense.

If you're not making sense to people, you're living YOUR life, not a prescribed one.

My wish for you is that you *never* make sense.

Acknowledgements

Where on Earth do I begin? Putting word art out into the world has been a life long dream, what surprised me more than anything is that it took on the form of poetry, but of course it did! Firstly, I must thank my husband for being so enthusiastically on board with this you could be forgiven for thinking I'd eliminated disease from the world. Theo, you are the biggest cheerleader I've ever had on my team and your belief in me both humbles and baffles me every single day. I love you.

Thank you to Harriette, who's equal belief in me lights a rocket underneath me daily. I'm genuinely unsure where I would be without your love, support, sisterhood and loyalty in my corner. I adore doing this human experience with you.

Thank you to the absolute rock star that is Chloe, my other Sanderson Sister and designer extraordinaire, you brought this book to life and captured the exact vision I didn't even know was in my head.

I can't wrap up this book without mentioning the exceptional Gwyneth Lesley, who shared her wealth of publishing knowledge and helped make the official existence of The Wisdom Life Gave You possible. Thank you for paving the way for dreams to come true and for seeing my words so deeply. Your recognition of what was unfolding created such a strong foundation.

And to you; that dream you had when you were a child, it still calls to you, doesn't it? Answer the call! Even if it's just for you, even if you only answer in a whisper. The world needs more dreams fulfilled and soul's expressed. Thank YOU in advance.

About The Author

Mia Burley is the debut author of the collection of poetry known as; *The Wisdom Life Gave You*. She has been writing professionally as a copywriter since 2012 and has also contributed many op-eds to local and national publications in the United Kingdom. She is known in the writing world for her emotive pieces and ability to connect to the reader in a deeply profound way.

As a typical Sagittarius she is completely allergic to routine and sticking to one thing only. In addition to her writing, she serves as the Managing Director and Head Life & Business Coach at the internationally acclaimed coaching company; Ask Harriette Ltd. She is also known as the Priestess of Presence and supports clients and loved ones with spiritual practices and principles for a life of healing and fulfillment.

She lives on the South Coast of England with her husband, who she loves just marginally more than the ocean!

@casaburley
https://www.instagram.com/casaburley/

www.ingramcontent.com/pod-product-compliance
Lightning Source LLC
Chambersburg PA
CBHW030440010526
44118CB00011B/725